Take Me Home

poems by

Sarah Levine

Finishing Line Press
Georgetown, Kentucky

Take Me Home

Copyright © 2020 by Sarah Levine
ISBN 978-1-64662-318-1 First Edition
All rights reserved under International and Pan-American Copyright Conventions. No part of this book may be reproduced in any manner whatsoever without written permission from the publisher, except in the case of brief quotations embodied in critical articles and reviews.

ACKNOWLEDGMENTS

My gratitude to the readers and editors of the following journals in which versions of these poems first appeared:

"Forgotten Things" *The Paris American*
"Her Man" *Elimae*
"Bag of Punches" *Passages North*
"Poodle" *Blaze Vox*
"I Want" *Whiskey Island*
"Bang-Bang" Winner of *Westchester Review* Writers' Under 30 Contest and 2017 MVICW Poetry Contest

Some of these poems were originally published in different variations within the chapbook *Her Man* from New Megaphone Press, 2014.

Publisher: Leah Maines
Editor: Christen Kincaid
Cover Art: Elise Ollman Kahle
Author Photo: Thomas Sayers Ellis
Cover Design: Elizabeth Maines McCleavy

Order online: www.finishinglinepress.com
also available on amazon.com

Author inquiries and mail orders:
Finishing Line Press
P. O. Box 1626
Georgetown, Kentucky 40324
U. S. A.

Table of Contents

1: Herman

Seeing Mother in Her Goodbye Box 1

With Begonia, After Mother's Funeral 2

Poodle 3

Her Man 4

Become 6

I Drive Days 7

Bang-Bang 8

Instant Hymn 10

Adultery 11

Left 12

I Want 13

Bag of Punches 14

Underwater Sky 15

Forgotten Things 16

Notes 17

For all my students:
near and far

1. Herman

Seeing Mother in Her Goodbye Box

It's easier to think of her cheeks pressed to a field
covered in white blossoms. The same field

that once held the footsteps of two dozen rabbits dusted in snow
or the turning carnival wheels last summer.

I want it to be last summer again, to watch the elephants' ears
become aprons in wind. When it got so hot everything

tasted like libraries dripping in gasoline. After the carnival
she stood inside the river finding fish to scrub into diamonds

while I pet the spine of her laughter
until it tangled itself into noose.

The rest of the summer I spent too much time
with hands covering all the holes that couldn't quit leaking

from my body. Now I cover myself in river
pray each scratch of sun will bruise enough color into my chest

to remind mirrors, how the living look.

With Begonia, After Mother's Funeral

I lie in the field
when the stars turn on

and fire tells the wood
what to say.

There is melon
in a bucket spit the seeds out

for planting and I want a bicycle.
A seat and wheels

to ride to the river until
I smell mother's dirty ghost

asleep in someone's garden.
And the neighbors never tell

when we steal begonia blossoms
to place behind each-others ears and run

through other peoples' backyards. Even this one time
when the rains begin and begin until our skin becomes wet

paper, and when spoken the three syllables
of your first name become a handshake with the rain

Poodle

You take the rings off your fingers and hold a peach pit on your tongue.
Your hair turns white in the sun, in the rain it turns poodle.

The sky is like an unreachable swimming pool and I wish I was a cloud.
I wish I was a storm cloud so I would be responsible

for turning your hair to poodle.
I try to speak and swallow a peach pit instead and you laugh laugh

And I hate you. I hate weather
moving through your lungs and I hate coughing lawnmowers.

I hate the way my lawnmowers scare birds back into the sky.
I hate the way you stand there, watching me thrash

like blade against field and I want to hurt you.
I want to steal sky in your mouth, bite your lips

until they swell like over-ripe watermelon.
I want to set a match inside your ear and watch your face bloom.

Her Man

1)
I am a terrible swimmer
All elbows and lungs.
But you—
Forearms swifter
Than slide trombones
Are song
Sweet-boned
Begonia—
Wet yellow braid
Caught in wind.
I know your noise
Belly full of fish.
I feel sorry for my shirts.
Mother sewed my name into each one
On the tag
Herman Herman Her Man.
Could I be?
Could I sew my name into your pocket?
Let my fingers brood and gasp.
I am jealous of the air between your knees
The dropped stitch on your hem.
The geese squawk like donkeys
And you turn toward them and their bugle throats
Mesmerized by the unrehearsed choir of wings.

ll)
I will pluck geese from the sky
Knock-kneed in fields of mint and pepper.
In rain when bones become spoons—
A throb song.
When the wings are quiet and smell of blown out candles
And you will kneel, feet bare
A wet prayer folding from your lips.
Let my lips
Listen into the shell of your ear—
Bony roads scattered with elms and white churches.

Become

In the rain you set your shoes free while your hair turned itself into wool and your dress became thin and your eyelashes became bristles and you held my hand and I asked my hand what to do I asked the clouds and seeds and shovel and you hung your dress on a stalk of wheat and I stopped asking

I Drive Days

Stay awake with bags of ice
behind my neck, heat

so loud, the world turns deaf.

Did I mention my new favorite sound is
bicycle gaining speed in rain.

Each raindrop
licking the throats of chimneys and school buses.

I stay awake with your name
dangling out of my open mouth, a worm
caught in weeds.

I still do not know the first lie

you ever told or why your laughter
reminds me of children running.

Bang-Bang

I went messy for Begonia.
Her gooseneck and hobnobbing.
How well she wears her white shoes and white socks.
She makes my tongue dumb
And when I lick her knees
I taste the heads of hammers.
I saw her first in mother's car
When she stepped through the street
In only the arms of a sweater.
My heart shot
Bang-Bang.
I couldn't stop licking the window clean.
I saw her second by the schoolhouse
Speaking to no one but the sky—
Air punches like bullets from a broken gun.
And I wanted to jump off my school desk and wrestle a thrush into her throat.
When I saw her third at mother's funeral
She put her hand inside my pocket
Smiled with teeth bigger than light bulbs.
And I felt clean like someone just threw me up into the world.
I am no longer a boy put together the wrong way.
I have a girl—
I have the girl who meets me under the trees
And lets me look close enough to see the hair on her chin.
My heart grows loud and messy.
And I realize I know nothing.
So I sock stalks of corn in the face until the sun has had enough.
I roll in puddles and plead for summer lightning to lift me off my feet
For I love you.
My hands and teeth and bloody pulp of a heart
Love you.
And I know one day you will leave me like mother.
I will stand over another goodbye box
The geese will rage beside the moon.

The books will grow inside the trees
And I will kneel close enough
To pick the hair from your chin.
Not yet.
Not today because your pockets are filled with peanuts.
You are making a jelly sandwich and spilling laughter
Into my throat—
Filling me the way a dozen thrushes fill a chimney.

Instant Hymn

I feel like straw
in the scarecrow.
When I am with you
I feel like straw
in the scarecrow in the rain,
in the mud
when dogs
chew each-other's ears
and storm
makes the grass grow.
I should touch the back
of your neck more.
Dance like a bucket
rolling down a mountain.
In the dark,
in the driveway
we stare at the moon,
pick fruit off a tree
and I want to
wash my hands less pulling red
birds out of each-other.
All heart and dirt
and everything would be new
because there is newness in the best things.

Adultery

Before the clouds brewed into storm
And the geese squawked into smoke
I stood watching his teeth
Unzip you free from dress
Inside your grandmother's trailer
And I became a terrible field
With too many farm tools
And a dog that pouts
Beneath the corn stalks shade
Trying to hide from a herd of flies
Never learning flies
Are everywhere

Left

You left my sheet in sweat

      The scent of a raccoon guarding her baby

Left the shadows of mulberry and mackerel

      How water feels without its town of fish

Left boats painted yellow and alligators with pimples on their cheeks

      Before I could dress myself in envelopes and stamp

Left sunflowers and cracked corn

      When the wind takes everything in its fists and blows the world blind

Left my mouth stupid

I Want

To become mutt with a paw's
quick stitch in the sand
longing to hold a fish.
To lick each gills'
flutter, invent song
made from instrument
of tongue and bite.
Send me out into
this world to outrun
a flock of rain knees
knocking so fast
my ears gust
back like candles
blown out by a child's
untaught breath.
I drink from garden
hose chase tricycles
into traffic and some

minutes even hear
My heart kick
like a can tossed

into a field
full of goats. Seeds
knock through my fur
and I am in love
with the girl
standing tip toe
selling corn
down the road. She
sweats sugar until mosquitoes
turn drunk.
She smells too ripe
too alive to be left alone.

Bag of Punches

By day I break glass and roll tires.
In this two-bite town, the boys grow into men and the men
grow back into campfire.
Take my money to the campgrounds
throw bread to the birds and wait for their stomachs to explode.
Can't drive past a wheat field without heart becoming bumper car
punching through a mountain.
By night, I sit on hoods of cars with hands that rise up and take--
names, wind, and bruises the color of plums cut open too late.
It feels good to be underestimated. To emerge from a cage
after wrestling the moon, sit on the edge of someone's swimming pool
and listen to a neighbor's daughter talk triumph in a body so beautiful
it makes me wince. I loved someone and you were just footsteps:
one punch, two kicks, three kisses.
You were born with a name only thunder could pronounce.

Underwater Sky

In day when I see the moon I think of you, I think about
what you are thinking about when you see the moon—a polar bear
holding up the sky. No. The stars hold up the sky. That's what mother
used to say in her wool gloves and dress
and I knew she was alive
when I could hear her boat heart swung in sea.
I still want to see the ocean. How big it really is, underwater sky
with shark and seahorse and shell.miss you
and your hands. If you asked them to touch me
they wouldn't recognize my face anymore.
I wish I still knew mother but she was carried out of church, marched
into the field where the cows kneel before rain. You are gone too—

Forgotten Things

Imagine you put your face against store windows
selling paper flowers and wooden horses.
You were made because two bodies forgot
risk, ignored recitation of kiss kiss tremble, a sermon
announcing the end of free love.
Love taught you to stand inside an ocean, feel the fish
smear their scales on wave after wave, all in the name of homecoming.
Love taught no manners,
fire set to someone's orchard so you become peach jam for days.
How absurd to be given a mouth that craves fruit bruised into sugar.
How easy it is now for you to chase chickens
wearing the reddest dress, legs running loud like forgotten pianos
being banged into existence.

Notes

"I Drive Days" is inspired from Corey Zeller's poem "Let's Get out of Here"

"Adultery" is after Jim Harrison

"Forgotten Things" is after Dean Young

Sarah Levine grew up in Wellesley, MA. Her poetry has been anthologized in *Best New Poets* and published in journals such as *Passages North, Green Mountains Review, Paris American, PANK, Fourteen Hills* among others. The recipient of fellowships and residencies from MVICW, Noepe Literary Arts Center, and Wellspring House, she has been nominated for the Pushcart anthology, won *Westchester Review's* Writers Under 30 Contest and is the author *Her Man* (New Megaphone Press, 2014). Levine is also a certified classroom educator. She won the Barnes & Noble Regional Favorite Teacher Contest and holds degrees from University Massachusetts Amherst, Sarah Lawrence College, and Smith College. She currently lives in Western MA and teaches at the Williston Northampton School.

www.ingramcontent.com/pod-product-compliance
Lightning Source LLC
LaVergne TN
LVHW041524070426
835507LV00012B/1803